POEMS AND PARADOXES

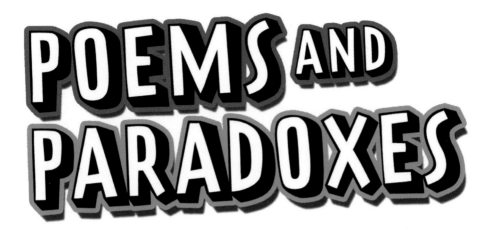

POEMS AND PARADOXES

KYLE. D EVANS

ILLUSTRATED BY HANA AYOOB

Tarquin

Book ISBN 978-1-91356-556-5
Ebook ISBN 978-1-91356-557-2
Design by Karl Hunt
Printed in the UK

Published by Tarquin
Suite 74, 17 Holywell Hill
St Albans AL1 1DT
United Kingdom

info@tarquingroup.com
www.tarquingroup.com

Kyle's Dedication

For Edwin & Juno x

Hana's Dedication

To my mother Mina, who was my first maths and art teacher. Thank you for encouraging my passion for drawing and numbers ever since.

Kyle's Acknowledgements

Thank you to Andrew at Tarquin for helping to make this project happen. Thanks to Hana for putting up with my ridiculous illustration requests ("can you draw a two that looks jealous?") Thanks to the families Inskip, Jeffs and Smith for giving me feedback throughout. Most of all, thank you to my family for their love and support.

CONTENTS

CONTENTS

1 | WHO SHAVES THE BARBER?

Here's a riddle a friend of mine found in their Christmas cracker:

What do you think? Is 'no' the answer to the question? Feel free to put the book down and have a little think about it.

Let's try out the two possibilities:

Is 'no' the answer to this question? **Yes!**

There is a contradiction here: if we answer with a 'yes', we're saying that we think 'no' is the answer to the question: but we just answered 'yes'.

Is 'no' the answer to this question? **No!**

Unfortunately here we are answering the question with a 'no', by which we're saying that 'no' is not the answer to the question. But we answered the question with a 'no'!

However you try to answer this question, you will be wrong. It's all very confusing, and it's meant to be: this is an example of what is known as a **paradox**. A paradox is a logically self-contradictory statement or set of statements. Here's another fun paradoxical question my son recently came up with: *what's smaller than nothing?*

A more famous example: imagine a village, and in that village imagine there is a barber shop. A rule of this strange village is that the barber shaves *only those villagers who do not shave themselves*. The question is, **who shaves the barber**? Again, you may wish to put the book down and have a think about it first.

Let us once again try out the two possibilities:

> *The barber shaves himself.* After all, he should be pretty good at shaving people! But if the barber shaves himself, then the barber is shaving someone who shaves himself, which breaks our earlier rule.

Someone else shaves the barber. Perhaps the barber gets his neighbour to shave him? If this is the case then his neighbour shaves someone who does not shave himself – but the barber is meant to be the only person who does that! We have arrived at another paradox.[1]

Again, this is meant to be frustrating and confusing. Here's a poem to maybe help you feel better about it all.

The barber's the friendliest man in the town
From the pauper in rags to the prince in his crown
And the shop-keeper hustling to earn every buck
To the lowly street-sweeper who's down on his luck
From the haughtiest priest to the clock maker's son
The barber takes time out to shave every one
Regardless of family, stature or wealth
He shaves every man who does not shave himself
There's only one question I harbour
Tell me please:
Who shaves the barber?

---

1   The above paradox actually gives us a useful analogy to an inherent flaw in set theory, and is often attributed to Bertrand Russell. That's a little beyond the scope of this book though!

The barber cares not for the size of your wage
Your caste or your creed or your background or age
From the college athletics team running their laps
To the pensioners fresh from their afternoon naps
And the inpatients dressed in their hospital gowns
He shaves every man in each part of the town
Regardless of attitude, wisdom or health
He shaves every man who does not shave himself
There's only one question I harbour
Tell me please:
Who shaves the barber?

2 | I DROPPED A PENNY IN A WELL

Here's a neat trick you can try next time you encounter a well – or any source of water that is directly below you – and want to know how far below you the surface of the water is:

1. Drop a stone, penny or other small object, and time how long (in seconds) after you release it you hear a 'splash'.

2. Take that time and multiply it by itself: this is called *squaring*.

3. Now take the new number you have and multiply it by five.

4. The number you now have is the distance between you and the water (in metres.)

For example, if you counted 3 seconds, the water is roughly $3 \times 3 \times 5 = 45$ metres below you. But why?

The key fact to know here is that any object dropped in any place on earth will **accelerate** towards the ground at approximately 10 metres per second per second. In other words, the velocity of the stone[2] increases by ten metres-per-second every second, starting from a speed of zero when the stone is held in your hand. So a graph of velocity against time for the example above would look like this:

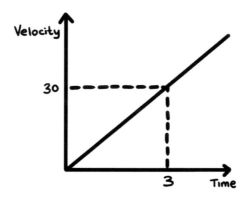

The area of the triangle under the graph represents displacement: the distance the stone has travelled since it was dropped. The area of a triangle is ½ × base × height, so in this case ½ × 3 × 30 = 45 metres.[3] Here's a little rhyme to help you remember this rule…

---

2   Speed and velocity mean the same thing as long as we agree in which direction we're measuring

3   Note, however, that the distance must be small enough for air resistance to be negligible – so no throwing a coin off the Empire State building and attempting to time its fall. You will also probably be arrested.

I dropped a penny in a well
And listened as the penny fell
And only when I heard a 'plop'
Did I let my stopwatch stop
The time it took to make its dive
I times'd that by itself, then five
And now – I hate to make you jealis -
I know just how deep the well is!

3 | I SPENT TEN POUNDS ON A ONE POUND COIN

How much would you be willing to pay for a one pound coin? Just a normal, regular one pound coin, not a special commemorative coin to celebrate Southampton winning the Premier League in 2022. You wouldn't be tempted to spend more than a pound, right? Not unless there were some special conditions, perhaps…

If you've ever been to an auction, witnessed one on TV or even bid for something on eBay, you'll know how an auction works. But just in case, here's an example:

Let's say you want to win an auction for a signed Ed Sheeran record,[4] and you're willing to pay £20 for it. The opening price is £10, so you bid £10, but another bidder is willing to pay more,

---

4   Because you just love how he names all his albums after mathematical symbols.

so they raise their hand and bid £15. The auctioneer asks if anyone is happy to bid £20 and you raise your hand and become the lead bidder again. But the auctioneer then asks if anyone is willing to pay £25 and your rival swoops in with such a bid. You are tempted to go on and bid £30 for the record, but you decide to step back at this point and concede defeat. Your adversary now owes the auction house £25 for the record, and you walk away empty handed, but still with the £20 you came with.

Now, back to our special £1 auction, in which all the rules are the same except for one: when you make a bid you are resigned to losing that money, *even if you don't end up winning*. So if you bid 50p for the £1 coin, but someone else outbids you, you still lose your 50p.

Perhaps you decide a safe way to win the £1 coin would be to bid 90p – that should see off any rival bidders, right? Sure you'd only come away 10p in profit, but it seems like a good strategy to win. But then a competitor swoops in and bids one pound, perhaps thinking it worth breaking even for the thrill of being the winning bidder.

What should you do next? Let's consider the two possibilities…

Option 1 – Stop bidding: If you stop at this point you will lose the 90p you bid.

Option 2 – Bid £1.10 for the £1 coin: If you do this you will be 10p in debt – you gain the £1 coin but it cost you £1.10 to get it, so you're now 10p in debt.

The two potential outcomes here are to be 90p out of pocket or 10p out of pocket. Clearly the second is preferable, so it is logically wiser to bid £1.10 for a £1 coin than to stop bidding.

However, your rival now finds themselves in the same boat – accept defeat and lose £1, or bid £1.20 and lose only 20p? It's a no-brainer! Where will this all end though?!

This head-scratcher of a paradox was created by the economist Martin Shubnik to show how a series of logical choices can lead to an illogical outcome. You may have noticed that the real winner here is the auctioneer, who takes home way more than a pound for the pound coin they are selling.

Think a little further, and it may also occur to you that the auctioneer could be defeated if all potential bidders acted together as a team, intentionally bidding low and then sharing their winnings. This is a nice introduction to **game theory**, a fascinating area of mathematics relating to the study of strategy and decision making, where what is best for the individual is rarely the same as what is best for the group as a whole.

I stepped into the auction hall
And nothing seemed unusual
The auctioneer stood to one side
And, "GOING, GOING, GONE!", she cried
The people sat – intentions hid –
With fingers poised to make their bids
And now and then the auctioneer
Would shout, "SOLD! TO THIS MAN DOWN HERE"

But here's where things turned somewhat strange
For suddenly, the rules had changed
"The next lot", said the auctioneer
"Is different, let me be clear
Each penny bid will then be lost
Regardless of the final cost
So if you bid and do not win
Your money's gone: let that sink in"

This change of rules seemed quite unfair
But soon, excitement filled the air
The auctioneer knelt to the ground
Then held aloft a shiny pound
(I sensed a bargain coming soon
And shuffled through the auction room)
Then she declared, mischievously,
"I start the bidding at 10p!"

I raced in with a 10p bid
What easier way to win a quid?
But then a man right next to me
Stood up and hollered "20p!"
Well, I bid 30 pence of course
Then he bid 40, in due course
The bidding war remained intense
'Til I had offered 90 pence

Now, have a think, what would you do
If you were in my rival's shoes?
To spend a pound to make a pound
Does not seem logically sound
But losing 80 pence is worse
Than having nothing in your purse
So he shouted "One pound!" and then
I pondered … and bid one-pound-ten

One-pound-ten for a one pound piece?!
That's madness! Foolishness at least!
But ten pence loss – think carefully -
Hurts less than losing 90p
See, one more bid, at any cost
Feels, somehow, like a lesser loss
My rival knew the same, and yet
We chased each other into debt

The gavel pounded! I had won!
It dawned on me what I had done…
There's no sense in what people buy
Even a careful chap, like I
By making steps quite logical
Had ended up a complete fool
Oh, what a crazy club I've joined -
I spent ten pounds on a one pound coin

4 | HOW BIG IS A HUNDRED?

Those of you who live in a house with a small person –
whether brother, sister, son or daughter – will be familiar with
the charming way they joyously string together nonsense
non-numbers of their own invention:

"Twenty hundred and thirty million thousand!"
"Thirteen hundred billionty million!"

(occasionally you might even hear politicians doing something
similar...)

It's entirely understandable that this happens though: big
numbers are difficult for anyone to get their head around, and
their names are quite abstract and easy to muddle up. When my
children get confused about the size of numbers, I try to come
up with mental pictures to help them. Sometimes it goes a bit
like this...

"How big is a hundred?" said little baby Win
How big is a hundred? Now where shall I begin…

A hundred tiddlywinks could make a square that's ten by ten
In a hundred days the seasons will have turned again
A hundred years: the time since England had a reigning King
A hundred pennies makes the pound the tooth fairy might bring
A hundred pounds to Mum or Dad is not a great amount
But a hundred pounds is more than many people ever count

"But how big *is a hundred?" said Baby Win, aghast*
Well, a hundred can be big or small: depends on who you ask

5 | SPARE A THOUGHT FOR SEVENTEEN

(Photo courtesy of Geoff Marshall, allthestations.co.uk)

The above picture is taken at an English railway station called Redcar British Steel, and as you can see from the image, things are not very busy there. In fact it is so quiet there that at the start of 2019 it was awarded the honour of 'Britain's least popular train station'.

Great news! The locals (all five of them) were very excited and put up a plaque to celebrate this fantastic achievement.

It made local and national news and tourists flooded[5] to visit the award-winning station. What was the result of this? The influx of visitors meant that Redcar British Steel lost its title as least popular station. That's right: by putting up a plaque to celebrate being the least popular station, it attracted more visitors, and hence had to take down the plaque!

I'm going to use a similar argument to attempt to convince you that there is no such thing as a boring number. Perhaps you already think so! But there will be times in life when you need to convince other people, and here's a way you can do it:

1. Assume the opposite: that some numbers are boring.

2. If there are boring numbers, there must therefore be a smallest boring number (say, 17, perhaps).

3. But being the smallest boring number surely is an interesting feature! So we can scratch that number off our list and move onto the next 'boring' number.

4. Now this next 'boring' number (say, 19) is the new smallest boring number, which in turn makes it interesting!

5. This process can be repeated indefinitely to show that, in fact, no numbers are boring.

---

5   OK, flooded may be a little strong: there were 360 entries and exits during 2018-19, still fewer than one per day on average, but up from just 40 the year before.

This is a somewhat tongue-in-cheek application of **proof by contradiction**, where we assume the opposite of what we are trying to prove and then show that this leads to an absurd or nonsensical conclusion. Serious mathematicians may baulk at such a mischievous use of an elegant, beautiful mathematical method. Luckily, I am not a serious mathematician.

Number one's the top dog
First position in a race
It takes two to tango
But try not to be two-faced
Three is father, son and ghost
Three wise men or three kings
Four seasons make up a year
From Summer through to Spring
Kids just love a high five
If they're five years old or younger
But spare a thought for seventeen
The smallest boring number

Six months at the gym
Would give your six-pack definition
Seven could be lucky
If you're into superstition
Eight great wonders of the world
Stand proudly in their cities

Maybe cats have nine lives
But don't test that claim on kitty
Humans count in tens
The digits with which we're encumbered
But spare a thought for seventeen
The smallest boring number

Eleven in a football team
From goalie to pen-taker
Twelve cakes make a dozen
(With a thirteenth for the baker)
The fourteenth day of February
Brings flowers, hearts and doves
Fifteen is a point in tennis
One point more than love
Sixteen bars are great for dancing
Foxtrot, jive or rhumba
But spare a thought for seventeen
The smallest boring number

*But seventeen, don't fret that there's no reason to
adore you*

*For you're just as exciting as all those that came
before you*

*You think you hold no interest but you overlook
one thing*

*Being the smallest boring number makes you
interesting!*

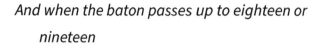

*And when the baton passes up to eighteen or
nineteen*

*Now they're not boring either: use the
argument just seen*

*So when somebody says, 'Numbers are
boring!' you can show 'em*

*They're wrong – not only that but you can
prove it with a poem*

6 | INFINITY BOTTLES ON THE WALL

Here's a common argument that any readers who grew up in a house with siblings might recognise:

"I hate you so much!"
> *"I hate you more!"*

"I hate you times a hundred!"
> *"I hate you times a million!"*

"I hate you times infinity!"
> *"I hate you times... infinity plus one!"*

If you haven't played the 'infinity plus one' card you have never truly argued. The trouble is, of course, that infinity plus one doesn't really mean what we might think it means. **Infinity**[6] is

---

6   Please note that in this chapter, strictly speaking the infinity I'm talking about is called *Aleph Null*, which is the smallest type of infinity. Yes, there are different sizes of infinity! But as long as we agree that whenever I write 'infinity' I mean the same size of infinity, it all works.

more of a concept than a number: something larger than any other countable number. You can't count to infinity, but when you count up and up in the traditional way you are heading *towards* infinity.

Infinity has some highly unusual properties when you try to do arithmetic with it. What really happens when you add one to infinity? First I ask you to imagine infinite empty bottles on an endlessly long wall (I hope you have a good imagination.) So the line of bottles starts where you are standing alongside bottle 1, and ends...well, it never ends.

Now let's say you found another bottle on the ground. Where would you put it? You can't walk it to the other end of the line – there is no other end! But you could call it bottle 0 and squeeze it onto the front. The line still extends from where you're standing (if you shuffle back a step) to some immeasurably distant point, so the line is actually just as long as it ever was: infinitely long! So adding 1 to infinity is still infinity. And this is only the start of the strange goings on when infinity meets arithmetic...[7]

7   This chapter and poem are really a tribute to 'Hilbert's Hotel', a genius thought experiment from the turn of the 20th century. I highly recommend looking it up – see Tarquin's book *Images of Infinity* – more at the back of the book.

Infinity bottles of beer on the wall
Infinity bottles of beer
You take one down, pass it around
Infinity bottles of beer on the wall!

I had infinity bottles of beer, I put them on my wall
I realised I'd left a bottle with my neighbour Paul
I took the extra bottle and I placed it at one end
Infinity plus one is still infinity my friend!

Infinity bottles of beer on the wall
Infinity bottles of beer
You take one down, pass it around
Infinity bottles of beer on the wall!

I had infinity bottles of beer, my boyfriend had the same
We placed them all upon our walls, it took all bleedin' day!

The line looked just as long when we placed them alternately
Infinity times two, therefore, is still infinity!

Infinity bottles of beer on the wall
Infinity bottles of beer
You take one down, pass it around
Infinity bottles of beer on the wall!

I found another friend who had infinite bottles too
We carried out the same trick, it was difficult to do
In fact, the same goes even if you had infinite friends
Infinity times infinity is infinity – the end![8]

---

8   Note: The green bottles are labelled alpha, beta, gamma, delta, the first four letters
    in the Greek alphabet.

7 | THIS ONE COOL MATHS TRICK WILL BLOW YOUR MIND!

You might be aware of square numbers, these are numbers that can be formed by creating squares of dots. So the first square numbers are 1, 4 & 9, as shown below:

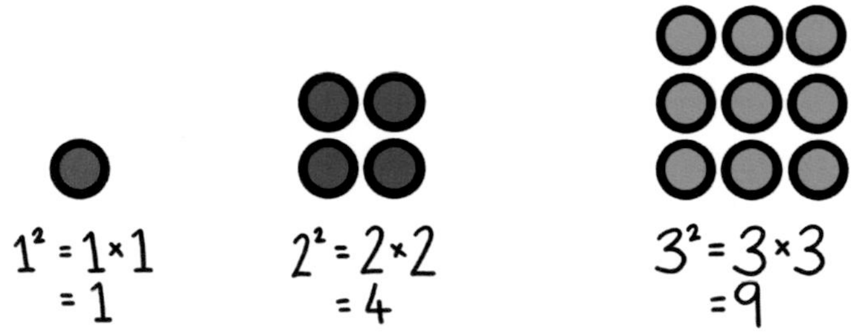

$$1^2 = 1 \times 1 = 1 \qquad 2^2 = 2 \times 2 = 4 \qquad 3^2 = 3 \times 3 = 9$$

So *squaring* 3 means calculating how many dots in a 3 × 3 square, or multiplying 3 by itself, like we did back when we were dropping a penny in a well. But what about if you wanted to square a number that isn't a whole number? Say your penny took 3 and a half seconds to hit the water: how would you calculate 3.5 × 3.5?

Your first instinct might be to do three-and-a-half lots of three-and-a-half, which you might do like this:

Three-and-a-half lots of three-and-a-half

= Three lots of three-and-a-half plus half a three-and-a-half

= (3 × 3.5) + (0.5 × 3.5)

= 10.5 + 1.75 = 12.25

Or you may have spotted that 3.5 lots of 3.5 must be halfway between 3 lots of 3.5 and 4 lots of 3.5:

1 × 3.5 = 3.5

2 × 3.5 = 7

3 × 3.5 = 10.5

4 × 3.5 = 14

So 3.5 × 3.5 is halfway between 10.5 and 14, ie 12.25.

BUT! There's a much more satisfying way of getting the same result: the number you intend to square, ie 3.5, is halfway between 3 and 4; multiply these numbers together to make 12, and then whack a 0.25 on the end.

3.5 × 3.5 = 3 × 4 + 0.25 = 12.25

This works for any number ending in 0.5! Check with your calculator if you don't believe me...

$4.5 \times 4.5 = 4 \times 5 + 0.25 = 20.25$

$5.5 \times 5.5 = 5 \times 6 + 0.25 = 30.25$

$6.5 \times 6.5 = 6 \times 7 + 0.25 = 42.25$

To see why this neat trick works, consider a square of dots that is 3.5 wide and 3.5 high.

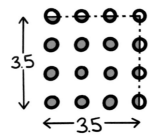

You could picture this as a 3 × 3 square with some extra half-dots and a quarter-dot. The half-dots go together to make 3 extra full dots. Then we must just remember the tiny orange quarter-dot, which is half of a half:

$$3.5^2 = 3 \times 4 + 0.25$$
$$= 12.25$$

By moving the half-dots all together and placing them at the top of the black 3 × 3 square of dots, we can form a 3 × 4 rectangle of dots. Pulling this all together, 3 × 4 + 0.25 = 12.25

A mathematician then wonders what would happen if you square *any* number that ends in 0.5: well, you would *always* get exactly enough half-dots to add a row to your rectangle, and you'd *always* be stuck with the poor old additional quarter-dot. So that means it will *always* work.

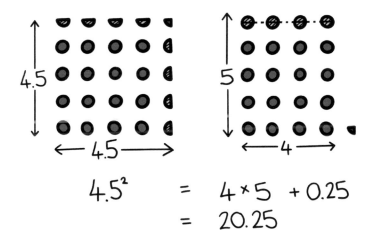

$$4.5^2 \quad = \quad 4 \times 5 + 0.25$$
$$= \quad 20.25$$

So to square any number ending in 0.5, simply multiply together the integers (whole numbers) either side, and put a 0.25 on the end!

When squaring a number that ends in a half
You may wander off down a difficult path
This one simple method might just blow your mind
(We've already shown that it works every time)

Just take the whole numbers that fall either side
Then multiply them and add nought-point-two-five
(Your smartphone could do this is two seconds flat
But honestly, where is the beauty in that?)

8 | HOW BIG IS A MILLION?

"How big is a million?" said little baby Win

How big is a million? Now where shall I begin...

A million seconds takes you to the middle of next week

A million years ago is way before humans could speak

A million people could lay down and sleep in Central Park

A million candle torch would help to keep away the dark

A million pounds would change your life

(But this might make you sour)

The richest man on earth earns that

In less than half an hour

"But how big is a million?" said Baby Win in awe

Well, a million can be big or small:

    depends on what it's for

9 | PARADOX OF TIME

If you drew a picture of the entire history of the world, from the beginning of time to its eventual end, it would look something like this:

*THE PRESENT

"Live in the present!", people will regularly tell you, but of course there's nowhere else you can live! By definition, the present is the tiny slither of time caught between the past (a whole load of stuff that has already happened) and the future (a whole load of stuff that's going to happen). But how tiny is that slither?

Does the 'present' mean the current day you're living in? It can't be: the day we're in contains some things that are in the past, like what you had for breakfast,[9] and some things that are in the future, like what you're going to read before bed.[10]

Maybe the present is the current minute you're living in. But in that minute you've read the word 'maybe' that started this paragraph (and is now in the past), and you're about to read the last word of this paragraph ('see') which is currently in your future (but by the time you've got there will be in your past – see!)

In fact any length of time, even a millisecond, can be broken down into parts. If it can be broken down, that means it has a beginning, middle and end, so it's too long to represent the present. So if any length of time is longer than the present, the present must have no duration. If it has no duration…that means the present doesn't exist. But we're in it right now! It appears we've hit another paradox.

---

9 Unless you're reading this before breakfast, well done if so.
10 Unless you're already reading this at bedtime, well done if so.

We might instead say that the present occupies an **infinitesimally** short space of time. It's definitely there, but any definable length of time you choose to describe it will be too long.[11]

The past is 13 billion or so years that have just gone
And most of it was really not that pleasant
The future reaches forward, stretching on and on and on
And the bit that's caught between is called the present
Try to trap the present in your fingers and you'll fail
It's the tiniest speck of time, crushed to its limit
It's infinitely small – infinitesimal, we say
And yet all that's ever happened, happened in it
And all these tiny moments, when you lay them head to feet
Reach from the dawn of time to where we're beckoned
An awful lot can change in one immeasurable beat
A life can change in much less than a second
And yet – here in a world where every moment's fresh and new
Some people follow old rules by the letter
The moment that you're in right now divides your life in two
So hold that moment tight
And make the second half the better

---

11 Using and understanding infinitesimals is a crucial step in some very important areas of advanced mathematics, including calculus, the study of change.

10 | DO THE FACTORIAL!

Here's a challenge for you. Imagine there are three items on your kitchen shelf: an apple, a banana and a carrot (yes, this is the kind of thing that tends to happen mostly in maths books.) Before you read on, try to work out how many different orders you could put the three pieces of food into.

As with any challenge in mathematics, the easiest way to make inroads into this problem is to simplify it. Say, for example, you only had one piece of fruit, an apple. Clearly there is only one order that you can sort your apple into. But if you then add a banana, there are now two orderings, or **permutations**, that your collection could be put into: the banana can slide in either after or before the apple, giving two permutations: AB or BA.

Next, somewhat inevitably, you add the carrot. There are currently two orders that you've achieved with your apple and banana – AB or BA – and for each of these orders there are three potential positions that the carrot could slot into: either to the far right, between the apple and banana, or to the far left. This gives three new orderings for each of the two previous permutations, totalling 6 new permutations: ABC, ACB, CAB, BAC, BCA, CBA.

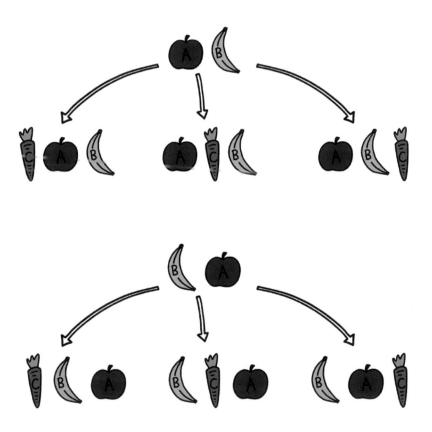

In summary:

Items:	Permutations:
1	1
2	$2 \times 1 = 2$
3	$3 \times 2 \times 1 = 6$

The operation observed in the right hand column – multiplying the number of items of fruit by every smaller number until you reach 1 – is called **'factorial'** and its symbol is an exclamation mark, so $3! = 3 \times 2 \times 1$, $4! = 4 \times 3 \times 2 \times 1$, and so on. Factorials have many uses in mathematics, often relating to situations involving probability.

Factorial numbers grow incredibly quickly, meaning that if you visited your local greengrocer and took one of every fruit or vegetable on sale, you would have no chance of living long enough to order them in every possible permutation. To give an idea of just how quickly factorials grow, try to guess the closest factorial number to the current world population. You might choose to pause here and have a guess before turning the page...

Startlingly, the world's population is just beyond 13! (that exclamation mark doubles both as the sign for a factorial and how amazing I find this fact to be.)

n	n!	Approximate population of…
1	1	
2	2 × 1 = 2	
3	3 × 2 × 1 = 6	
4	4 × 3 × 2 × 1 = 24	
5	5 × 4 × 3 × 2 × 1 = 120	
6	6 × 5 × 4 × 3 × 2 × 1 = 720	Mid-sized school
7	7 × 120 = 5040	Small village
8	8 × 5040 = 40,320	Small town
9	9 × 40,320 = 362,880	Nottingham
10	10 × 362,880 = 3,628,800	Uruguay
11	11 × 3,628,800 = 39,916,800	Canada
12	12 × 39,916,800 = 479,001,600	South America
13	13 × 479,001,600 = 6,227,020,800	Earth

Ok, 13 factorial is about a billion short of the world population. But 14 factorial would be 14 times bigger still, certainly many times bigger than the Earth's population will ever reach.

Yet another way of thinking about it: if everyone in the world stepped out onto the street and grabbed the nearest person, then these pairs moved into threes, then these new groups of two threes got themselves into fours, and so on, by the 13th grouping almost everyone in the world would be involved....

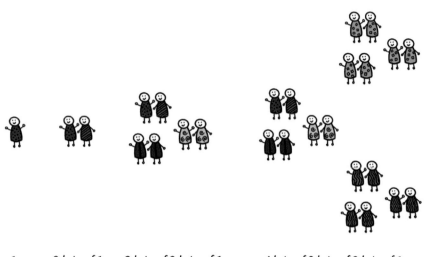

| *1* | *2 lots of 1* | *3 lots of 2 lots of 1* | *4 lots of 3 lots of 2 lots of 1* |

It's time to put on your dancing shoes
Link hands with your partner and dance in twos
Other hand in the air, like you just don't care
Everybody in the world's dancing in pairs

Now take these pairs and group into threes
(You can do this part with relative ease)
Not a problem on earth this dance can't fix
With the whole world dancing in groups of six

When these new groups move into fours
You'll probably need to step outdoors
The whole world moving like a dream
With 24 dancing in every team

There'll barely be space to waltz or jive
When the twenty-fours move into groups of five
'Cos five times four times three times two
Makes 120 in every crew

Now continue the pattern through larger sets
See how big factorial numbers get
You'll see, by the thirteenth iteration
One dance for the whole world's population

'Cos 13 times 12 times 11 times 10
Times 9 times 8 times 7, and then
Times 6, 5, 4 times 3, times 2
Makes 7 billion (give or take a few)

Imagine that – in thirteen moves
The whole world locked in a single groove
It's unlikely to work, I fear
But, hey
It was a nice idea

11 | HUNTING BEGHILOS

0.7734

If I've confused you by starting the chapter with that number, perhaps it would help if I wrote it with an old-fashioned calculator display:

0.7734

Still none the wiser? Try turning the page upside down…

The word 'hello' is a **beghilo**, that is, a word that can be written upside-down on an old-fashioned calculator. They are called 'beghilos' because such words have to consist only of the letters B, E, G, H, I, L, O and S.[12]

---

12 And also Z at a stretch. Oh, and you need to use a decimal point when words need to end with an O.

In Beghilo land, Santa arrives to the sound of 5773846l375, chuckling 0.40404. Here in the real world, the rock band The Hollies released an album in 1979 called 53l7704. Dutch readers might enjoy doing the calculation 14149 × 5166.

Beghilos were a cause of great amusement when I went to school, but these days hardly anyone has a calculator that actually works for Beghilos. Find a calculator in your house now, and I bet 0.7734 upside down doesn't look like HELLO. It certainly won't on your phone calculator.

This poem is my attempt to preserve Beghilos in the 21st century. To fully enjoy it you'll have to turn the book upside down whenever you encounter a Beghilo. I enjoy thinking of some of you reading this book in public, and wondering what the hell people watching you will think you're doing as you constantly rotate the book by 180 degrees.

Ready to go? Let's go on a Beghilo hunt…

We're out hunting 50714638, there's little time to 3507
You cannot find a 0.714638 in gardens or in 5002
Put on your hunting 5376606, pack your 49l375 in case of
    snow
We're out hunting 50714638 – ready, steady, 0.6!

Of all my favourite 5318804, this one fills my heart with 3376
Because a wild 0.714638 is quite a thing to 335
Keep your footwear sensible, I wouldn't bring 573344614
At any time we might need run from 35336 or 5604 or 5733

Hop the 607! Through the 608! As the water 5345075
If you need to keep your 53045 dry, pop on your 53450706
When we need our 5317738 full we'll rest our weary 5637
But what's that in amongst the 531717… 400! 0.714638 5663!

44444445.....

4506! A 0.714638 has seen us! 345 foresaw our 36315!
Now 5345 really angry and she 535514, time to leave!
We couldn't catch a 0.714638 but we had fun, no 5537
I'm glad we've had a 376616, but that's all – good night, god
  55378

12 | FRED THE LAZY FROG

Imagine you're sharing the last biscuit in the tin with your best friend: we've all been there. You break the biscuit in half, eat half and pass the other half to your chum. But your friend has a pang of guilt about eating the last of it, and decides to break their half into two, passing half of their half (that's a quarter of the original biscuit) back to you. But now you feel guilty too! So you do the same...

This is getting quite hard to explain now, so here's a diagram to show the process. For the sake of keeping things as simple as possible I've assumed that the original biscuit is a perfect square, and that my friend and I can break biscuits perfectly in half.

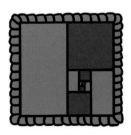

You can see your parts in light brown and your partner's in dark brown.[13] This diagram is a nice way of introducing yourself to a very important mathematical idea: that of a **limit**. The biscuit will never actually be entirely eaten if my partner and I keep halving what's left of it, but the amount of biscuit left over will certainly get closer and closer to zero, or, *infinitesimally small*. That means that it is definitely there, but any amount of biscuit you chose to represent the infinitesimal part would definitely be too big – a bit like choosing a length of time to describe the moment we live in.

So it follows that ½ + ¼ + ⅛ + ... = 1, where the dots can be replaced by an infinite number of smaller and smaller fractions. Or more accurately:

$$\sum_{n=1}^{\infty} \frac{1}{2^n} = 1$$

Meaning that as you add more and more fractions, each of which is half the size of the previous, you will get closer and closer to 1, without actually ever getting there. Is it frustrating that an infinite amount of something can add up to less than 1? If so, I know someone who will empathise . . .

---

13 Bonus challenge: it's obvious that I will end up with more biscuit than my friend, but can you find the eventual proportion of the biscuit that I will end up with? For the answer see page 76.

Fred was a frog, and a very, very lazy frog
A very lazy frog: no less, no more
He started the day with a really-quite-enormous jump
But every jump from there: half the one before

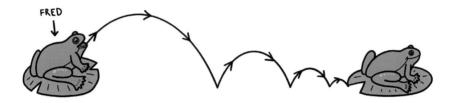

He starts the day jumping to the end of the fish pond
His following jump's half a fish pond less
'Til he grinds to a halt in the middle of the morning
It causes his mother no end of stress:

"Why can't you be simple like uniform Ewan?
Your little baby brother, he's the talk of town
So what if his jumps are just one millimetre?
He gets where he's going and he never slows down

"Or maybe you could hop like oscillating Oliver
Who jumps to the left, then jumps to the right,
Then further to the left, then further to the right again
Until he ends up jumping out of sight!"

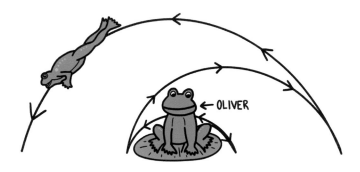

Fred wandered homeward (in ever smaller jumps, of course)
Thinking to himself – it's not my fault!
I step off my lily pad and really try hard
But by twice my first jump I come to a halt

But the saddest thing of all comes to Fred quite suddenly
Now, if his first jump was a metre, say
And after his first jump he had to pop home again
He'd never get home if he jumped all day!

See a half, plus a quarter, plus an eighth, et cetera
Adds up to one… but a little bit less
Which leaves the fat frog stuck just off his lily pad
Poor old Fred, what a terrible mess

13 | WHERE DO ALL THE NUMBERS GO?

"Buongiorno! This is my sister Juno and she loves frozen peas!"

The above is a sentence that my son once said to our neighbour. Do you think anyone else has ever said that sentence in the entire history of the earth? Obviously thousands of millions of people have walked the earth, constantly in conversation with each other. But the three specifics – the relatively rare girls' name, unusual food choice and Italian greeting – surely make the odds pretty low that anyone else has ever said this particular sentence.

I've thought about this phenomenon many times in my life: all the myriad strings of common words that no-one has ever put together yet, but one day might. Similarly I've also often wondered: how many numbers are there that have never yet been used?

There are infinitely many whole numbers, or integers, stretching off into infinity just like the bottles on the wall we met previously. And even though billions upon billions of numbers great and small have been used by humans, this is still a **finite** amount. Because there are infinitely many integers, and finitely many that have ever been used for anything, that means there are *definitely* integers that have never been used by anyone. Actually, there are infinitely many numbers that have never been used – and that's before we even get to all the fractions and decimals that fall between the whole numbers!

I can't help but feel sorry for those numbers that have been sitting around since the dawn of time, just waiting for their day in the sun.

Where do all the numbers go when they're not being used?
What becomes of all the seventeens and forty-twos?
They hang out in a giant hallway, safe from our detection
Stretching to infinity (plus one) in both directions

Numbers like one-eighty are just sitting on the shelves
Feeling sad that school children don't learn their fifteen
*   twelves*
But one hundred and eighty leaves the shelf for action plenty
When someone at the darts world cup obtains three treble
*   twenties*

Where do all the numbers go when they are not in action?
What becomes of all the decimals and surds and fractions?
They wait in an enormous hall, away from prying eyes
(And numbers that are complex reach up high into the skies)

Some numbers keep getting picked, others are hardly used
Really, it's enough to give a decimal the blues
Old Three-point-one-four-one-five-nine is quite a lonely guy
But has to sit right next to Mr Popular (that's Pi)

Where do all the numbers go? It's difficult to tell
Remember, for each number there's a negative as well
Like tickets at the deli counter waiting to be called
If someone calls their name out loud they get to leave the hall

But since the shelves are infinite and our choices are strict
It follows there are some numbers that never will be picked
So each number you've ever heard of, whether big or small
Should really be quite grateful it got off the shelf at all

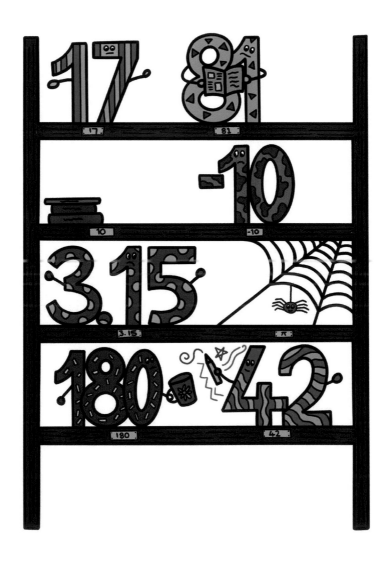

14 | MILLION, BILLION, TRILLION

Million, billion, trillion – why do they sound the same?
I think we should call a billion by a different name
A beezlenut, a babadook, even a bazzlebizz
Then we might see a billion pounds for just how much it is

A billion one pound coins would be much heavier than your house
The stack of coins would make Mount Everest cower like a mouse[14]
If I gave you a pound a second (this will drive you mad)
When you had earned a billion you'd be old as mum or dad

A billion people live their lives on just a pound a day
There are two thousand billionaires, or, put another way
If all the billionaires would get together, eye to eye
They certainly could change the world – if only they would try

---

14 Actually this stack of coins would easily reach into space! I'll let you do the maths...

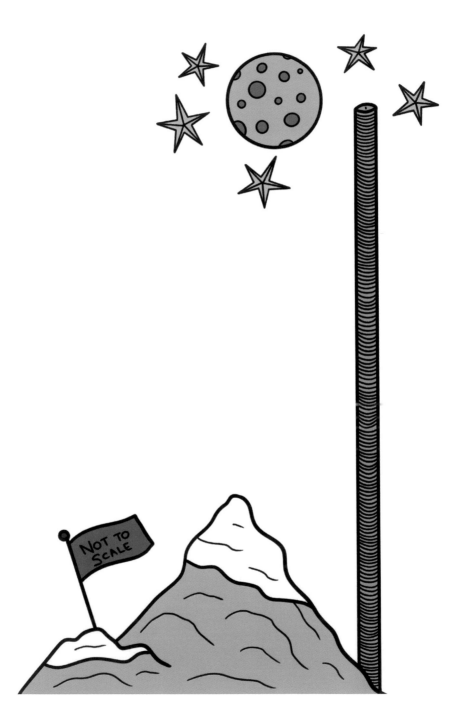

15 | IT'S GERMAIN'S WORLD

The fact that you're holding this book – and have got this far through it! – suggests that you might be a lover of mathematics. Many people love mathematics because it's a universal language: it's the subject you'd be most likely to understand if you were thrust into a classroom in a foreign country where you didn't know the language. It's based on pure logic and it doesn't care about your politics, your race or your gender.

Well, actually that's not entirely true. Things are certainly better than they used to be, but it wasn't all that long ago that things were very different. How many mathematicians could you name if I gave you thirty seconds? You might even like to give it a try by turning the book over and saying the names out loud.

Who said Pythagoras?

Newton?

Einstein?

Who named a woman?

I'm ashamed to say I got all the way through degree level maths without knowing the name of a single non-male mathematician of note. I'm even more ashamed to say that I thought this was because men were just better at maths. The truth is that until a hundred years or so ago, it was frowned upon, or even illegal, for women and girls to do mathematics. In many cultures it still is. Here is the story of Sophie Germain[15] (1776-1831), a brilliant mathematician who had to create a secret male pseudonym to be allowed to do maths at all, defying both her own family and the educational establishment.

---

15 Pronounced jer-MAN, that's important for the rhyming later...

I must confess it's alarming
Here in 18th century France
Where a woman must foremost be charming
Be quiet, polite and to dance
So I've been considering lately
It surely can't be that unique
For a woman to want more than babies
To read, write and actually speak
Yet here I am under a bedsheet
A candle to light up my work
I make calculations in private
My parents think it some odd quirk
Since I'm made to feel like a bad girl
For finding mathematics a joy
It seems I was born in a man's world
I might have more luck as a boy

Now I've become so knowledge-hungry
I'd spend every centime and franc
Since French universities shun me
I'll call myself 'Monsieur Le Blanc'
Just men can request notes from lectures
And make correspondence by mail
So I shall avoid the inspectors
Monsieur Le Blanc surely can't fail!

I need to somehow pass my workings
To maybe Lagrange or to Gauss
Then I might do proud maths in public
Not locked in a cage like a mouse
Society thinks me a mad girl
For having the courage to try
But since I was born in a man's world
I'll do what I can to get by

I'd thought about going to lectures
Dressed up in some man-like disguise
Try hard to fit in with the others
Tell man-jokes while slapping my thighs
But Gauss liked my methods and called me
I hardly could turn up in drag
He said: 'this imbalance appals me'
The cat was now out of the bag
Lagrange and Gauss fought in my corner
Now there was no hiding for me
But though I did great mathematics
A girl couldn't get a degree
You might live in less of a man's world
But always try not to forget
Not long ago it was Germain's world -
You might have a way to go yet

IT'S NICE
TO BE NICE

My next door neighbour Peter wants to take some of my garden

I looked at neighbour Peter and I said: 'I beg your pardon?'

He said 'I only want a tiny corner for my daughter

She wants to plant this seed she found

She says she'll keep it watered'

I've never seen his daughter but perhaps she'll come to visit

A tiny patch of grass is really not a big ask, is it?

So I gave it to him gladly and I heeded Mum's advice:

You should always trust a neighbour

Because it's nice to be nice

My neighbour Peter knocked again and this he had to say:

'I'd simply like as much again as I took yesterday

I need to park my bicycle, I can't keep it indoors

Besides, your garden's massive, you could give a little more'

Now personally, I didn't think my garden all that big

I was hardly hosting football games or farming sheep and pigs
But I think I've said it once before, and now I've said it twice
Good things come back to good people
Because it's nice to be nice

My neighbour Peter knocked again and now I'm sensing trouble
As every time I grant his wish, the land he takes is double
First he wanted one, then two, then four, then eight square metres
I'm starting to think no amount will be enough for Peter
He's burnt the grass with barbecues, the rest has gone to weeds
I hope that soon he'll have all of the garden that he needs
One day I'll have to stop this or someone will pay the price
But for now I let him have it
Because it's nice to be nice

So now the place is ruined, I'm sliding towards my fate
I love my house and yard but everyone says it's too late
My neighbour's ripped the garden up to park his seven cars
My children can't believe I ever let it get this far
And now he's forced the door open and wants to get inside
This is the final chance I have – I must not be denied
This is my only home, I can't let someone else live in it
It is nice to be nice, yes
But there has to be a limit

The Biscuit Question

Here's the answer to the question posed on page 60.

First you take a half and your partner takes a quarter, so you take twice as much as them. Then you take an eighth and your partner takes a sixteenth, so you take twice as much as them again. This will continue for as long as you play the game, so you always take twice as much as your partner. If you take twice as much as your partner, you must take two thirds of the biscuit, and your partner takes one third.